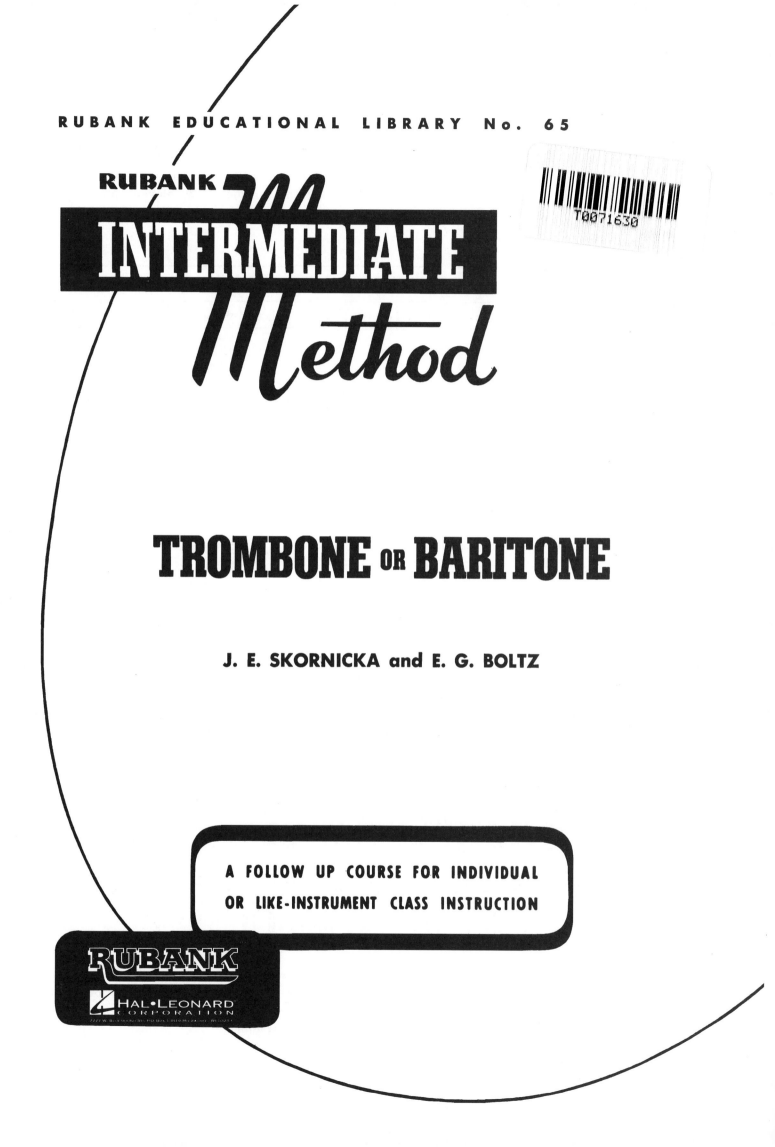

RUBANK EDUCATIONAL LIBRARY No. 65

RUBANK
INTERMEDIATE
Method

TROMBONE OR BARITONE

J. E. SKORNICKA and E. G. BOLTZ

A FOLLOW UP COURSE FOR INDIVIDUAL
OR LIKE-INSTRUMENT CLASS INSTRUCTION

RUBANK
HAL•LEONARD
CORPORATION
7777 W. Bluemound Rd. P.O. Box 13819 Milwaukee, WI 53213

Chart of Slide Trombone Positions
and Baritone Fingerings

The air within a trombone or baritone (or any other instrument with a cup mouthpiece) may be made to vibrate as a whole or in fractions of its length by varying the tension of the player's lips. The various pitches thus produced in each of the seven slide positions (and valve combinations) are indicated in the following table:

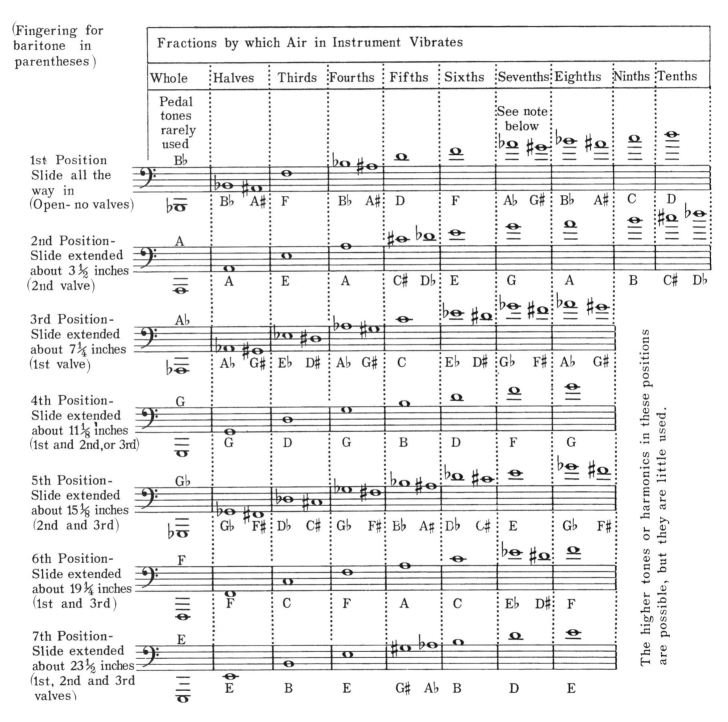

NOTE: All tones produced by the air vibrating in sevenths are flat and must be corrected by making the position for that tone about an inch shorter. This, of course, is impossible in 1st position on trombone and in all fingerings on baritone. The baritone player must chose a different fingering for the required tone or force it into tune with his lips. The latter is seldom satisfactory.

ESSENTIAL PRINCIPLES
of
Good Instrumental Performance

GOOD TONE is necessary in order that one's playing be pleasing to the listener as well as the player. Good tone can be produced only when the instrument is in good playing condition, equipped with the correct type of mouthpiece and played with the correct embouchure.

INTONATION: When two successive tones of different pitch are produced, it is necessary that each tone be in tune with the other, relative to the interval being played.

TUNE: The player must develop and train his ear so that a difference of pitch can be distinguished when playing with others.

NOTE VALUES: The player must develop a rhythmic sense so as to give proper value to tones as represented by the written notes.

BREATHING AND PHRASING: Each is usually dependent on the other. Since teachers of wind instruments differ on the methods of breathing, no special method is advocated, but it soon becomes evident to all players that in order to get good musical phrasing, it is necessary to breathe properly and in the proper places of a composition. It will be to the pupil's advantage to spend much time and effort on this phase of playing and take seriously all suggestions given by the teacher.

EXPRESSION MARKS: Expression marks in music are considered just as important as punctuation in prose and poetry. Good phrasing is the performance of music that has been properly punctuated. Expression marks put character into a mass of notes and if properly observed, will produce satisfying musical effects.

RELAXATION AND PROPER POSITION OF BODY AND HANDS: Whether playing in standing or sitting position, it is necessary that the body be erect and relaxed. Relaxation is the secret to the accomplishment of success in many other professions and trades. The arms must be relaxed, the elbows away from the body and the hands assuming a restful position on the instrument.

SUFFICIENT TIME FOR PRACTICE: Since different pupils require different types and lengths of practice periods, the objective that every pupil should establish is : "I will master the assigned task whether it takes 1/2 or 2 hours." The accomplishment of a task is far more important than the time that it consumes.

PROPER CARE OF THE INSTRUMENT: Carelessness in the handling of an instrument is the most prevalent handicap to the progress of young players. No pupil can expect to produce good results if the instrument is in poor playing condition. The instrument must be handled carefully and when a disorder is discovered, have it remedied immediately. Constant attention as to the condition of an instrument will pay dividends in the end.

MENTAL ATTITUDE OF TEACHER AND PUPIL: In order that the musical results be satisfactory, both the pupil and teacher must be interested in their task, and must have a perfect understanding of what that task is. The teacher must understand the learning capacities of the pupil so that the pupil in turn will get the type and amount of instruction that he will understand and be able to master.

J. E. S.

234-264

3

1. Have the instrument in good mechanical condition, namely, valves well moistened or oiled and slides properly lubricated.

2. One of the important essentials in the performance of music is a sound rhythmic conception. When this conception is established, correct playing will result at sight.

3. In playing the succeeding studies, special attention must be placed on the proper adjustment of the embouchere. Not all players are able to attain the same type of embouchere, but the one that produces the best and easiest results must be discovered by both the teacher and student.

4. Rhythms in this lesson are fundamental, and their mastery will make playing fluent and comprehensive.

5. A quick shift of the slide in trombone playing is essential at all times. Think of throwing the slide when shifting away from first position and of rolling it back when shifting it toward first position. The slide should stop for every tone regardless of how fast or how slow the passage.

Trombone positions appear below the notes.
Baritone fingerings appear above the notes.

NOTE AND REST VALUES

The various sections of this lesson are concerned not only with notes but with rests as well. It is just as important to be able to count and feel rests as it is to play and feel the notes.

MARKS OF EXPRESSION AND THEIR USE

PIANISSIMO .... *pp* ....Very soft   FORTISSIMO .... *ff* ....Very loud

PIANO .... *p* .... Soft   FORTE .... *f* .... Loud

MEZZO PIANO........ *mp* ....Medium soft   MEZZO FORTE.......*mf*........ Medium loud
(Normal tone)

In playing a tone on a brass instrument, unless otherwise marked, it should be held at the same level of volume, or in other words, the volume should not increase or diminish. This type of a tone will be indicated by means of parallel lines, thus: ========== The distance between the parallel lines will be a guage as to the difference of volume to be used.

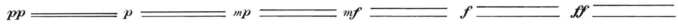

DAILY LONG TONE STUDIES

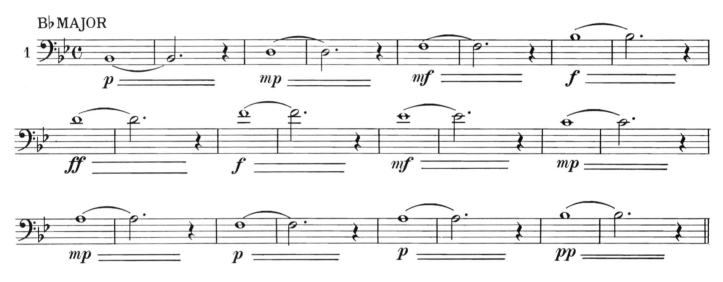

The following exercise should be played daily. Think of a big tone when playing this exercise. Practise it at the beginning of each practice period.

STUDIES IN EXPRESSION
Sound Graduations

Crescendo (cresc.) Gradually louder   Decrescendo (decresc.) or Diminuendo (dim.) Gradually softer

In playing a crescendo or a diminuendo the pitch of the tone must not be changed. It is a common fault of especially young players, to play flat when playing loud and sharp when playing softly.

In order to play the sound graduations or nuances correctly, it is necessary that the quality of the tone is not affected, but retain its rich and mellow fullness. ONLY THE VOLUME SHOULD CHANGE.

When a note is followed by one or more shorter notes, the shorter notes are played with one half the volume of the longer note. There are exceptions to this rule, but it is a good policy to learn to play all phrases as mentioned, since the majority of all music played in this way will be properly performed. Players interested in the fundamentals of solo playing will be greatly aided by adhering to this principle.

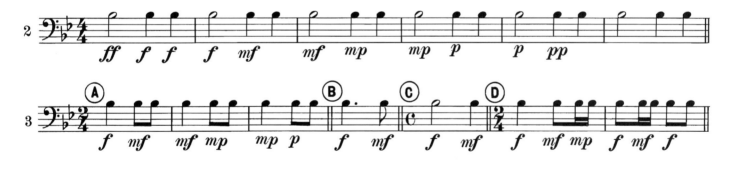

★
BLUE BELLS OF SCOTLAND

★ Using lines No. 2 and No. 3 as patterns, write in the various volumes required for each note and measure. This will acquaint the player with the sound graduations necessary in the playing of simple songs.

Legato Study

The expression marks as indicated in all music are actually a part of that music and considered as important as the notes. To use expression marks even at the first reading of new music is a good habit to acquire.

LEGATO (with auxiliary positions for trombone)

SOLO – GLIDING

Eb MAJOR   C MINOR (*Melodic*)

Etude Expressivo

Play all notes with full volume.

ETUDE EXPRESSIVO

Accents

The rinforzando ($>$) is placed over a note for the purpose of bringing out that particular tone more strongly than the other tones in the same sequence. The rinforzando or accent punctuates the important notes of a measure or sequence.

WALTZ

MARCH

ACCENT ETUDE

Crusader's Hymn

Traditional

NOW THE DAY IS OVER

BARNBY

Staccato Studies

As written

As played

1

LIGHT TONGUING ETUDE

Moderato

2

f

simile

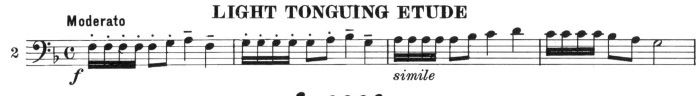

MELODY

Moderato

3

mf

simile

(♭)

CHORD ETUDE

Allegro

4

f

simile

5

5

5

Staccato Etudes

CHORD STUDY

STACCATO TONGUING ETUDE

Rapid Scale Study

STACCATO AND QUICK SHIFT ETUDE

WALTZ

SCALE AND CHORD DRILL

LEGATO ETUDE

Scale and Chord Studies

SUMMARY STUDY

Scale and Interval Studies

SCALE ETUDE

STACCATO ETUDE

Bb MAJOR

G MINOR (*Melodic*)

Minor Studies

Eb MAJOR SCALE

C MINOR SCALE. (*Harmonic*) 7th step raised ascending and descending.

C MINOR SCALE. (*Melodic*) 6th and 7th steps raised ascending. Normal tones descending.

ETUDE IN C MINOR

Moderato

simile

ETUDE IN G MINOR

Andante

simile

There's Music in the Air

GAVOTTE IN F MAJOR

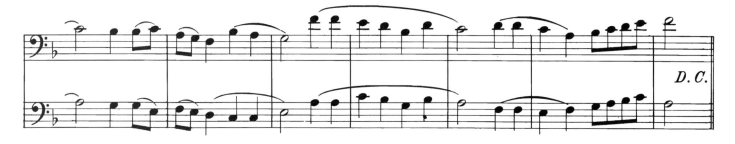

Syncopation

₵ SYNCOPATION

2/4 SYNCOPATION ETUDE

6/8 Rhythm

RAPID SLIDE SHIFT ETUDE

ETUDE for LEGATO and STACCATO PLAYING

Triplet Studies

MELODY IN 6/8 TIME

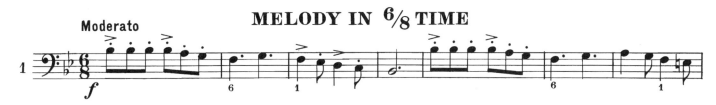

MELODY IN 2/4 TIME

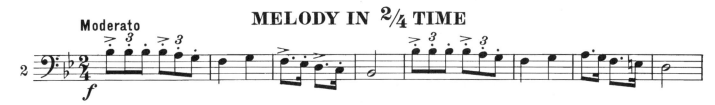

MELODY IN 12/8 TIME

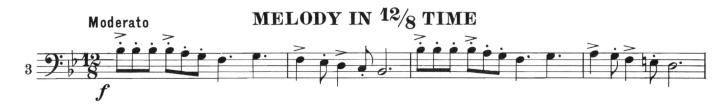

TECHNICAL ETUDE

A♭ Major Studies

STACCATO INTERVAL STUDY

LEGATO STUDY

F MINOR SCALE (*Melodic*)   (*Harmonic*)

Lip Slurs

When two successive notes of different pitch are slurred without the change of valves or slide, it is called a lip slur. Lip slur exercises will appear in many of the succeeding lessons and are intended for the purpose of developing lip flexibility, strengthening the muscles of the lips and face. At first the muscles of the face will tire rather quickly, but with daily practice will become strong and flexible thus making the playing cleaner and easier. Do not hinder the flexibility of the lips by pressing them too tightly against the mouthpiece. Daily practice of lip slurs is the procedure followed by all good pro - fessional brass instrument players.

Chromatic Studies

CHROMATIC MELODIES

Then You'll Remember Me

From the Opera "Bohemian Girl"

BALFE

LULLABY

BRAHMS

Articulation Studies

Rhythmic pattern

Rhythmic pattern

FOLK DANCE

Allegro

1

LIP SLUR ETUDE No.1

Moderato

3

LIP SLUR ETUDE No.2

Moderato

4

Dotted Eighth Note Studies

DOTTED EIGHTH NOTE STUDY

Moderato

1

JOY TO THE WORLD

Christmas Carol

Moderato

2

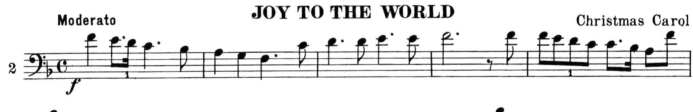

INTERVAL STUDY

Moderato

3

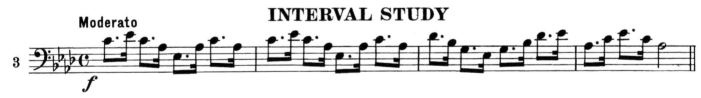

OH TANNENBAUM

Andante

4

Chord and Scale Studies

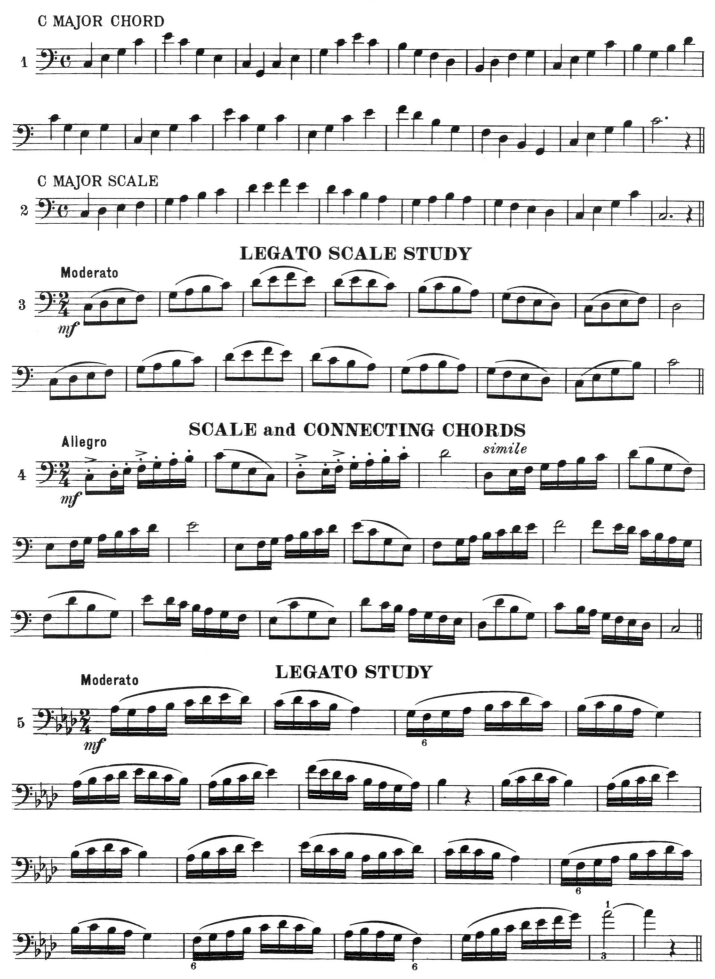

Memories
Waltz

In swinging style - *Legato*

1

Rubato

WHEN YOU AND I WERE YOUNG

Andante

2

Fine

D.C.

To beginning

G Major Studies

G MAJOR SCALE STUDY (Legato)

LIP SLUR STUDY

LEGATO SOLO

CHORD AND ACCENT STUDY

E MINOR SCALE (*Melodic*)

Rhythmic Development

MELODY IN 6/8 AND 3/4 TIME. No.1

No.2

RELATIONSHIP OF 6/8 AND 3/8 TIME

ALLEGRO IN 3/8 TIME

Tempo di Valse

Technical Studies

Duet

Allegro moderato

1

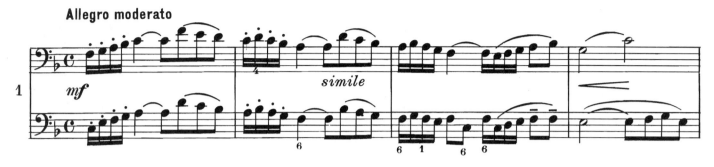

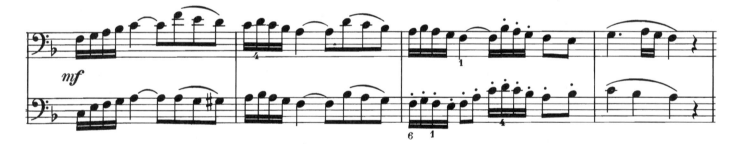

WALTZ

Tempo de Waltz

2

Syncopation Studies

Articulation Studies

LEGATO AND STACCATO ETUDE in C MAJOR

Db Major Studies

Db MAJOR SCALE

1

Db MAJOR CHORD STUDY

2

LONG LONG AGO

Andante

3

BLUE BELLS OF SCOTLAND

Moderato

4

ETUDE IN Db

Moderato

5

G♭ Major Studies

G♭ MAJOR CHORD

G♭ MAJOR SCALE

LONG LONG AGO

Andante

RAPID TONGUING ETUDE

Allegro

Moderato

Scale and Chord Etude

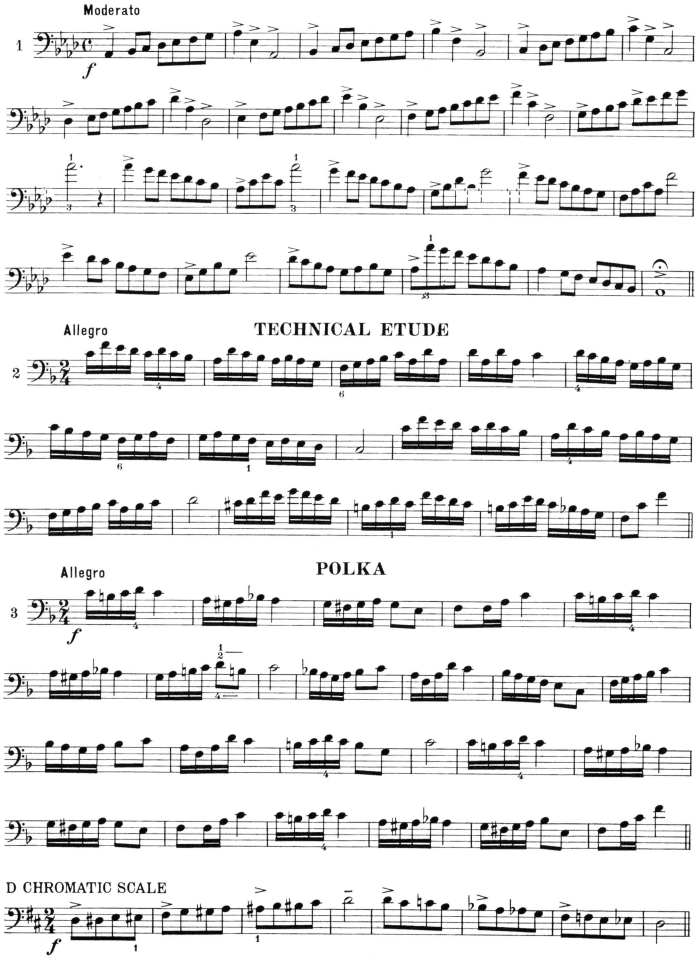

TECHNICAL ETUDE

POLKA

D CHROMATIC SCALE

Technical Studies

INTERVAL AND SCALE ETUDE No.1

ETUDE No.2

ETUDE No.3

Dotted Eighth Note Studies

ETUDE No.1

Scale Studies

No.1

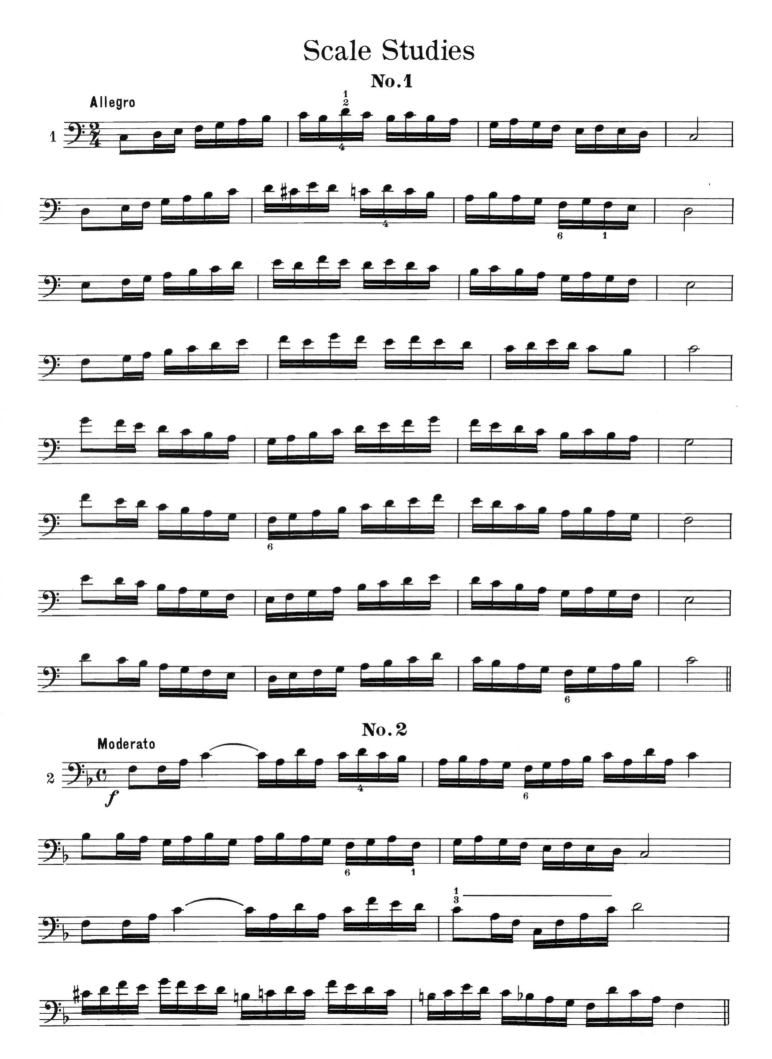

Chord and Interval Etudes

ETUDE No.1

ETUDE No.2

ETUDE No.3

ETUDE No.4

Eb CHROMATIC SCALE

Sharpshooter's March

METALO

Allegro

In the Gloaming

HARRISON

Slowly

Steal Away

Negro Spiritual

Duet Brilliante

Major and Relative Minor Scales

Major and Relative Minor Scales